MARKETING SUCCESS SECRETS

Practical tips to skyrocket your online sales

Ray Goodwin

CONTENTS

LIABILITY DISCLAIMER

The information contained within this book is intended for informational purposes only and should not be construed as legal or professional advice. The authors and publishers of this book are not responsible for any losses or damages that may arise from the use of the information contained within.

The reader assumes full responsibility for any decisions made based on the information in this book. The authors and publishers do not endorse any particular method, service or product mentioned in this book and are not responsible for any consequences resulting from their use.

The reader should exercise caution and discretion when making life changing decisions, and should be aware of the risks and potential consequences of their actions. This book is not a substitute for professional or legal advice and should not be relied upon as such.

By reading and using the information in this book, the reader acknowledges and agrees to hold harmless the authors, publishers, and any other parties involved in the creation or distribution of this book from any and all liability, claims, damages, or losses that may arise from their use of the information contained herein.

CHAPTER 1: SETTING YOUR FOUNDATION FOR MARKETING SUCCESS

Welcome to Marketing Success Secrets! In this book, I will share with you my extensive knowledge and experience in online sales and marketing. Over the past 25 years, I have seen many trends come and go, but one thing remains constant: the importance of effective marketing.

Marketing is the backbone of any successful business. Without it, you cannot attract customers or generate revenue. In today's digital age, there are countless ways to market your products or services online. From social media ads to email campaigns to influencer partnerships, the options can be overwhelming.

That's why I've written this book - to help guide you through the maze of modern marketing techniques and show you what really works. But more than that, I want to inspire you to think outside the box and create your own unique approach to marketing.

Throughout these pages, you'll find practical advice on how to optimize your website for search engines, create engaging content that resonates with your target audience, build a strong brand identity across all channels, and much more.

So whether you're a small business owner trying to increase sales or a marketer looking for fresh ideas, Marketing Success Secrets has something for everyone. Let's get started!

Marketing

Marketing can seem overwhelming at first glance, with countless channels and strategies to choose from. However, the key to success lies in a strong foundation built on a few core elements. In this chapter, we will discuss the foundational elements essential to any successful marketing plan.

Defining Your Target Audience

The first step in building a strong foundation for successful marketing is to define your target audience. Who are you trying to reach with your message, and what are their demographics, interests, and behaviors? Without understanding your audience, it's impossible to effectively tailor your marketing message to their needs and desires.

Creating a Unique Selling Proposition

Once you know who your audience is, you need to define your unique selling proposition (USP). A USP is the key benefit that sets your product or service apart from competitors and solves a specific problem for your target audience. Your USP should be concise and compelling and guide your messaging across all marketing channels.

Establishing Measurable Goals

Setting measurable goals is vital to determining the success of your marketing efforts and ensuring that you are moving toward your business objectives. Goals should be specific, measurable, achievable, relevant, and time-bound (SMART), enabling you to track and adjust your progress over time.

Developing a Budget for Marketing Activities

Marketing requires an investment of resources, including time, money, and people. Developing a budget for your marketing activities helps ensure that you are allocating your resources effectively and getting a positive return on your investment.

Building a Strong Brand Identity

A strong brand identity is a crucial foundation for any marketing plan. Your brand identity should embody your business's values, personality, and unique selling proposition. It should be consistent across all marketing channels and materials, including your website, social media profiles, and print materials.

Conducting Market Research

Market research involves gathering and analyzing data about your industry, competitors, and target audience to better understand their needs and behaviors. Research can provide valuable insights into what your customers want, what your competitors are doing, and where there may be gaps in the market.

Understanding Your Competitors

Knowing your competitors and their marketing strategies is essential to standing out in a crowded market. By analyzing their messaging, positioning, and tactics, you can identify gaps in the market and opportunities to differentiate your business.

Choosing the Right Marketing Channels

With so many marketing channels available, it can be challenging to prioritize. Choosing the right channels for your business depends on your target audience, goals, and budget. Some channels may be more effective for brand awareness, while others may be better suited for driving conversions.

By focusing on these core foundational elements, you can build a strong base for your marketing plan and set yourself up for success. In the following chapters, we will dive deeper into specific strategies and tactics to help you achieve your marketing goals.

CHAPTER 2: CRAFTING YOUR MARKETING MESSAGE

Your marketing message is the foundation of your brand identity. It's what sets you apart from competitors and defines your unique selling proposition. Crafting a clear and compelling message is crucial for reaching and resonating with your target audience. In this chapter, we will explore the key elements of crafting a successful marketing message.

Communicating Your Brand's Story

Every brand, like any individual, has a unique story to tell. Your brand's story is what helps customers understand who you are, what you do, and why you do it. It's important to craft a compelling brand story that resonates with your target audience to establish a connection and build trust. Your brand's story should be authentic, memorable, and consistent with your overall message.

Creating Compelling Headlines and Taglines

A headline or tagline is the first thing that your audience will see and should instantly grab their attention. It should be clear and concise, and convey the message that you want to convey. Creating a memorable and engaging headline or tagline requires creativity and a deep understanding of your target audience. It should reflect your unique selling proposition and differentiate you from your competitors.

Perfecting Your Elevator Pitch

Your elevator pitch is a brief, attention-grabbing overview of your brand that's delivered in the time it takes to ride an elevator. A well-crafted elevator pitch should convey your brand's value proposition, uniqueness, and key messaging. It's an essential tool when pitching your brand to potential investors, customers, or partners. Your elevator pitch should be clear, concise, and tailored to your audience.

Identifying Your Core Messaging Pillars

Your core messaging pillars are the key messages that define your brand identity and differentiate you from your competitors. These messages should be consistent across all marketing channels and campaigns. Identifying your core messaging pillars requires a deep understanding of your target audience, your brand's value proposition, and what sets you apart in the marketplace.

Focusing on Benefits, Not Features

When crafting your marketing message, it's important to focus on the benefits you offer to your customers, not just the features of your products or services. Benefits are what your customers care about, and what ultimately drives purchasing decisions. Focusing on benefits helps you connect with your customers emotionally and communicate the value you offer.

Incorporating Storytelling into Your Marketing

Human beings are wired to respond to stories. Incorporating storytelling into your marketing is a powerful way to connect with your audience emotionally and build trust. Your brand's story and customer stories should be woven into all of your marketing efforts to create a lasting impression and more effective messaging.

Using Emotional Triggers to Connect with Your Audience

Emotions are a powerful tool in marketing. When you connect with your audience emotionally, you create a stronger connection and build trust. Emotional triggers can include happiness, fear, joy, sadness, anger, and more. Identifying the emotional triggers that resonate with your audience can be a key differentiator for your brand.

Crafting a Consistent Message Across All Marketing Channels

Crafting a consistent message across all marketing channels is critical for building a strong brand identity and establishing credibility. Your messaging should be consistent across all marketing channels, including email, social media, advertising, and more. Consistency in messaging helps to drive recognition and trust in your brand.

In conclusion, crafting an effective marketing message requires a deep understanding of your target audience, your brand's unique selling proposition, and how to communicate that value in a way that resonates emotionally. Creating clear, consistent, and compelling messaging can set your brand apart from competitors and drive long-term success.

CHAPTER 3: LEVERAGING SOCIAL MEDIA FOR MARKETING SUCCESS

Social media has become an integral part of our lives, and businesses have realized its potential for reaching customers and building long-lasting relationships with them. With over 3.8 billion social media users worldwide, social media offers businesses of all sizes the opportunity to connect with their audience, promote their brand, and drive sales. However, many businesses struggle to leverage social media effectively, and this can result in wasted time, resources, and opportunities.

Choosing the Right Social Media Platforms for Your Business

The first step to successful social media marketing is to choose the right social media platforms for your business. With so many platforms available, it can be overwhelming for businesses to decide which platforms to use. Before you choose your social media platforms, you need to consider your target audience, the goals you want to achieve, and the type of content you plan to share.

Facebook is the largest social media platform, and it's suitable for businesses that target a wide range of audiences, including B2C and B2B. Twitter is ideal for businesses that want to communicate with their followers in real-time and share updates about their services or products. LinkedIn is perfect for B2B businesses looking to connect with professionals in their industry. Instagram is suitable for businesses that want to showcase their products visually, while Pinterest is ideal for businesses that want to share tips, ideas, and inspiration.

Developing a Social Media Strategy

Once you have chosen your social media platforms, the next step is to develop a social media strategy. A social media strategy outlines the goals you want to achieve, the content you plan to share, the frequency of your posts, and the metrics you will use to measure success. Your social media strategy should align with your overall marketing goals and should be flexible enough to adapt to changes in your business environment.

Creating Engaging Content for Social Media

Social media is all about engaging content that resonates with your audience. The content you share should be informative, entertaining, and useful. It should also align with your brand values, tone, and personality. Some types of content that work well on social media include images, videos, infographics, blog posts, and user-generated content. By creating engaging content for social media, you can attract new followers, retain existing ones, and increase engagement on your posts.

Building a Community of Followers and Fans

One of the keys to success on social media is building a community of followers and fans. To do this, you need to engage with your audience, respond to their comments and messages, and share content that resonates with them. You can also run social media contests, offer exclusive promotions, and feature user-generated content to build a sense of community and loyalty.

Utilizing Paid Social Media Advertising

While organic social media marketing is great, businesses can also use paid social media advertising to reach a wider audience and drive sales. Paid social media advertising allows businesses to target specific audiences based on demographics, interests, and behavior. By using paid social media advertising, businesses can increase their reach, drive traffic to their website, and generate leads.

Measuring the Success of Your Social Media Efforts

To ensure the success of your social media marketing efforts, it's essential to measure your results regularly. You can use metrics such as engagement rate, reach, click-through rate, and conversion rate to evaluate the effectiveness of your social media marketing strategy. By measuring your social media metrics, you can identify areas that need improvement, adjust your strategy accordingly, and optimize your social media marketing efforts.

Staying Up-to-date with Social Media Trends and Changes

Social media is constantly evolving, and it's essential to stay up-to-date with the latest trends and changes. You can do this by attending social media conferences, following social media influencers, and subscribing to social media blogs and newsletters. By staying up-to-date with social media trends and changes, you can stay ahead of the competition, identify new opportunities, and adapt your social media marketing strategy accordingly.

Avoiding Common Social Media Mistakes

Many businesses make common social media mistakes that can

hurt their efforts. Some of these mistakes include ignoring negative comments, using too many hashtags, posting irrelevant content, and not responding to messages promptly. To avoid these mistakes, businesses need to have a clear social media strategy, be consistent in their posting, and engage with their audience regularly.

Conclusion

Social media offers businesses of all sizes the opportunity to connect with their audience, promote their brand, and drive sales. By choosing the right social media platforms, developing a social media strategy, creating engaging content, building a community of followers, utilizing paid social media advertising, measuring your metrics, staying up-to-date with trends, and avoiding common mistakes, businesses can leverage social media effectively for marketing success.

CHAPTER 4:
SEARCH ENGINE OPTIMIZATION (SEO) STRATEGIES FOR SUCCESS

Search engine optimization, commonly known as SEO, refers to the practices that are used to increase visibility and improve the ranking of a website or web page on search engine result pages (SERPs). SEO is essential for businesses looking to attract organic traffic to their website and increase their online presence. In this chapter, we will discuss the fundamentals of SEO, how to conduct keyword research, strategies for optimizing website content and building backlinks, and how to monitor and analyze SEO performance.

Understanding the Fundamentals of SEO

Search engines like Google and Bing use complex algorithms to crawl and index websites and web pages. These algorithms take into account various factors such as keywords, content relevance, backlinks, website speed, and user experience, among others, to determine the ranking of a website or web page on SERPs.

Search engines prioritize websites and web pages that provide high-quality content, are mobile-friendly, and are easy to navigate. SEO aims to optimize these factors by making website and web page content more accessible and relevant to search engine algorithms.

Conducting Keyword Research

Keyword research is a critical component of SEO, as it helps businesses understand what their target audience is searching for and what keywords or phrases they should be targeting to improve their online visibility.

To conduct keyword research, businesses can use online tools such as Google Keyword Planner, Ahrefs, and Moz. These tools provide insights into the search volume, competition, and potential cost per click for different keywords and phrases.

When conducting keyword research, it is essential to focus on long-tail keywords, which are more specific and have lower competition than broad keywords. Long-tail keywords usually consist of three or more words and provide better targeting opportunities for businesses.

Optimizing Website Content for Search Engines

Once businesses have conducted keyword research, they can optimize their website content to target these keywords and improve their online visibility.

Some ways to optimize website content for search engines include:

- ❖ Including relevant keywords in website content, headings, and meta descriptions

- ❖ Creating high-quality, informative content that provides value to visitors

- ❖ Making website and web page content easily accessible and organized

❖ Optimizing images and videos with alt tags and captions

It is also essential for businesses to ensure that their website is mobile-friendly, as search engines prioritize mobile-friendly websites when ranking search results.

Building High-Quality Backlinks

Backlinks, or inbound links, refer to the links that other websites provide to a business's website or web pages. Search engines use backlinks as a way to assess the authority and relevance of a website.

Building high-quality backlinks is therefore an essential component of SEO. To build backlinks, businesses can engage in link building activities such as guest posting, outreach, and broken link building. Businesses can also create high-quality content that naturally attracts backlinks from other websites.

Utilizing Local SEO Tactics

Local SEO refers to the practices that businesses use to improve their online visibility in local search results. Local SEO is especially critical for businesses that rely on foot traffic, such as brick-and-mortar stores.

Some ways to utilize local SEO tactics include:

❖ Listing the business on Google My Business and other local business directories

❖ Optimizing the website and web page content with local keywords and phrases

❖ Building high-quality backlinks from local websites

❖   Creating locally focused content such as blog posts and landing pages

Optimizing for Mobile Devices

Mobile devices now account for a significant percentage of all online searches. As such, it is essential for businesses to optimize their websites and web pages for mobile devices to improve their online visibility.

Some ways to optimize for mobile devices include using a responsive design, reducing page load times, and optimizing images and videos for mobile devices.

Monitoring SEO Performance

Monitoring and analyzing SEO performance is crucial for businesses looking to improve their online visibility and attract organic traffic to their website.

Businesses can monitor their SEO performance by using tools like Google Analytics, which provides insights into website traffic, user behavior, and conversion rates.

To analyze SEO performance, businesses can track website and web page ranking on SERPs, monitor backlinks and referring domains, and track changes in website traffic and user behavior.

Keeping Up with Changes in Search Engine Algorithms

Search engine algorithms are constantly changing, and businesses must keep up with these changes to maintain their online visibility.

Staying up-to-date with changes in search engine algorithms requires continuous learning and adaptation. Businesses can attend industry conferences and webinars, subscribe to relevant newsletters and blogs, and engage with industry experts on social media to stay informed about changes in SEO best practices and strategies.

Conclusion

SEO is an essential component of digital marketing, and businesses must optimize their website and web page content for search engines to attract organic traffic to their website and improve their online visibility. By conducting keyword research, optimizing website content and building backlinks, utilizing local SEO tactics, and monitoring and analyzing SEO performance, businesses can improve their SEO strategy and drive success in their digital marketing efforts.

CHAPTER 5: CONTENT MARKETING FOR BUSINESS SUCCESS

Content marketing has become an essential aspect of business success in the modern marketing world. It has completely changed the way businesses interact with their audience. The aim of content marketing is not to promote products or services directly but to provide value to the customer by creating informative, engaging, and valuable content that addresses their needs.

Creating a content marketing strategy

The first step in content marketing is creating a content marketing strategy. This strategy should align with your business goals and objectives and should focus on creating content that is relevant to your target audience. The strategy should also identify the specific types of content that will be produced, the platforms on which it will be shared, and the frequency of content production.

Developing a content calendar

Once you have a content marketing strategy in place, it is important to create a content calendar that outlines the specific types of content that will be produced and the publication schedule. The content calendar helps to ensure that the content is aligned with your business goals and that it is produced in a timely manner.

Writing engaging blog posts and articles

Blog posts and articles are the most common types of content produced in content marketing. They are an excellent way to provide valuable information to your target audience. When writing blog posts and articles, it is important to ensure that the content is informative, engaging, and easy to read. Ideally, it should provide a solution to the reader's problem and should be based on the target audience's interests, pain points, and needs.

Producing high-quality video content

Videos have become increasingly popular in content marketing. They are highly engaging and can be used to provide more in-depth information on a specific topic. When producing video content, it is important to ensure that the content is high-quality and relevant to the target audience. It should be short, concise, and visually appealing.

Utilizing infographics and visual content

Infographics and visual content are excellent ways to present complex information in a visually appealing way. They are highly shareable and can increase engagement with your target audience. When producing infographics and visual content, it is important to ensure that the content is relevant, accurate, and easy to understand.

Developing lead magnets and downloadable resources

Lead magnets and downloadable resources are an excellent way to attract potential customers and collect their contact information.

These resources can be in the form of white papers, e-books, or case studies. When creating lead magnets and downloadable resources, it is important to ensure that the content is highly valuable and provides solutions to the reader's problem.

Promoting your content effectively

Producing high-quality content is not enough if it is not promoted effectively. There are several ways to promote content, including social media, email marketing, and paid advertising. It is important to promote content on the platforms where your target audience is most active. This will increase engagement and drive traffic to your website.

Analyzing the success of your content marketing efforts

Finally, it is important to measure the success of your content marketing efforts. This can be done by tracking metrics like website traffic, engagement, and conversion rates. These metrics will help you determine which types of content are most effective and how to optimize your content marketing strategy for better results.

In conclusion, content marketing plays a crucial role in business success in the modern marketing world. By providing informative, engaging, and valuable content to your target audience, you can increase engagement, drive traffic to your website, and ultimately increase conversions. It is important to develop a content marketing strategy, produce high-quality content, and promote it effectively to achieve the best results. Measuring the success of your content marketing efforts will also help you optimize your strategy for better results.

CHAPTER 6: EMAIL MARKETING FOR MAXIMUM IMPACT

Email marketing is still a powerful marketing tool that can help businesses connect with their customers and drive sales. In this chapter, you will learn how to build an email list, craft compelling email content, and utilize segmentation and personalization to maximize the impact of your email marketing efforts.

Building an email list

The first step in email marketing is building an email list. There are several ways to achieve this, but the most effective method is through permission-based email marketing. This involves asking for permission to send promotional emails to customers and prospects who have opted-in to receive them.

One way to build an email list is to offer an incentive in exchange for an email address, such as a free e-book or discount code. Another way is to include a call-to-action (CTA) asking visitors to your website to sign up for your newsletter or promotional emails.

Crafting compelling email subject lines

Once you have built an email list, the next step is to craft compelling email subject lines. The subject line is the first thing that recipients see when they receive an email, so it is crucial to make it interesting and engaging. An effective subject line should be short, attention-grabbing, and convey the value of the email content.

Creating engaging email content

The content of your emails should provide value to your audience. This can include promotional offers, helpful tips and advice, or industry news and updates. The key is to keep your content relevant and interesting to your audience. It's also important to maintain a consistent tone and branding in your email content to reinforce your brand identity.

Utilizing segmentation and personalization

Segmenting your email list based on demographics, behavior, or interests can help you tailor your email content for maximum impact. Personalization can also help increase engagement by addressing recipients by name and tailoring content to their specific needs and preferences.

A/B testing email campaigns

A/B testing involves sending two versions of an email to a small subset of your email list and measuring the response to see which version is more effective. This can help you optimize your email content and subject lines for maximum impact.

Incorporating calls-to-action (CTAs)

CTAs are an essential component of email marketing and can help drive conversions. A clear and compelling CTA encourages recipients to take action, whether it's to buy a product, register for an event, or visit a website.

Analyzing email open and click-through rates

Measuring the success of your email marketing efforts is crucial for continuous improvement. Open and click-through rates provide valuable insight into the effectiveness of your email content and subject lines.

Avoiding common email marketing mistakes

There are several common email marketing mistakes that should be avoided, such as sending too many emails, using spammy subject lines or content, and failing to provide value to your audience. It's also important to ensure that your emails are optimized for mobile devices, as more and more consumers are accessing email on their smartphones and tablets.

Conclusion

Email marketing can be an effective tool for businesses to connect with their customers and drive sales. By building an email list, crafting compelling subject lines and content, utilizing segmentation and personalization, incorporating CTAs, and analyzing email performance, businesses can maximize the impact of their email marketing efforts. Avoiding common email marketing mistakes can help ensure that your emails are well-received and effective.

CHAPTER 7: PAY-PER-CLICK ADVERTISING TO DRIVE RESULTS

In today's digital age, it's crucial to have a strong online presence to compete in the market. Pay-per-click advertising can be a valuable tool in achieving this. PPC advertising is a model of online advertising where advertisers pay each time a user clicks on one of their ads. With PPC advertising, businesses can drive traffic to their website and increase conversions.

Understanding the Fundamentals of Pay-per-Click Advertising

Before we dive into the intricacies of PPC advertising, let's first understand its fundamentals. PPC advertising allows businesses to bid on specific keywords or phrases relevant to their target audience. When a user enters those keywords into a search engine, the ad with the highest bid will appear at the top of the search results. This allows businesses to have their ads seen by potential customers who are actively searching for products or services they offer.

Choosing the Right PPC Platform for Your Business

To determine which PPC platform is right for your business, you need to understand the differences between the three most popular: Google Ads, Bing Ads, and social media advertising.

Google Ads is the largest and most popular platform, accounting for over 70% of all PPC advertising. Bing Ads, on the other hand, offers cheaper cost-per-click rates. Social media advertising, such as Facebook Ads and Instagram Ads, allows businesses to target specific demographics with an array of ad formats.

Developing Effective Ad Copy and Visuals

The ad copy and visuals play an important role in PPC advertising. The copy should be concise and compelling enough to catch the user's attention and encourage them to click through to your website. It should also include a call-to-action that tells the user what action to take next.

The visuals should be visually engaging and relevant to the copy. The color scheme should align with your brand identity to build brand recognition and trust.

Conducting Keyword Research and Targeting

Keyword research is vital for PPC advertising. Advertisers must conduct thorough research to determine the most relevant keywords and phrases that their target audience is searching for. Advertisers can then bid on these keywords to appear on the top of search results.

Managed bids and budgets

PPC advertising works based on a bidding system where businesses bid on keywords that they want to target. Advertisers need to manage their bids and budgets carefully to ensure they get the best ROI from their ad spend. If the bids are too low, their ads may not appear at the top of search results, whereas if the bids are too high, they may end up paying more than they would like.

Monitoring and Adjusting Campaigns

PPC advertising requires constant monitoring and adjustment to ensure it is achieving the desired results. Advertisers need to monitor their campaigns regularly to identify any underperforming ads and adjust bids accordingly.

Tracking and Analyzing PPC Performance

It's imperative to track the performance of PPC advertising campaigns to make data-driven decisions. This data enables advertisers to make tweaks to their campaigns and optimize the performance of their ads.

Maximizing ROI Through PPC Advertising

To maximize ROI, businesses need to start by setting clear goals that align with their overall marketing strategy. It's important to measure campaign performance using metrics such as click-through rate, conversion rate, cost per click, and cost per acquisition.

It's also essential to optimize campaigns. This means adjusting bids, changing ad copy, and visuals, and targeting different audiences to improve click-through rates, conversions, and overall ROI.

Avoiding Common PPC Advertising Mistakes

PPC advertising can be a valuable tool for businesses, but mistakes can be costly. Common mistakes include bidding too much or too little, choosing the wrong keywords, creating poorly written ad copy or visuals that are not relevant to the target audience. It's important to carefully plan campaigns, conduct thorough research, and monitor performance to avoid making these mistakes.

Conclusion

PPC advertising can be a powerful tool to help businesses achieve their marketing goals. By choosing the right platform, developing effective ad copy and visuals, conducting thorough research, managing bids and budgets, tracking performance, and optimizing campaigns, businesses can create successful PPC advertising campaigns that drive traffic to their website, increase conversions and boost ROI.

CHAPTER 8 – PUBLIC RELATIONS FOR BUSINESS SUCCESS

Public relations or PR refers to the process of managing and maintaining a positive image and reputation of a business or an individual. PR is all about building relationships with the public and the media. A solid PR strategy can help businesses to increase brand awareness, establish credibility, and create a positive brand image.

Crafting a Public Relations Strategy

The first step to a successful PR campaign is to craft a strategy that aligns with your business goals. Before you begin, it is important to identify your target audience and understand the kind of information they are interested in. A good PR strategy starts by identifying clear objectives that will guide all your PR activities.

Once your objectives are in place, focus on identifying key messages or storylines that align with your brand identity and business values. Your messaging should be consistent and should resonate with your target audience. The next step is to determine your media outreach strategy. The media can help to amplify your messages and increase your reach. This includes identifying the appropriate media outlets to target, building relationships with journalists, and developing a content calendar.

Developing Media Contacts and Relationships

Building relationships with journalists and other media outlets is a critical component of a successful PR strategy. As you identify the media outlets that are relevant to your business, it is important to build relationships with their editorial staff and journalists. This means reaching out to individual writers and editors to introduce yourself and start a conversation.

As your relationships with journalists and other media professionals grow, look for opportunities to collaborate and provide useful information. This can include sharing industry insights, providing background information on your business, or simply connecting journalists with other industry experts. Good media relationships take time to develop, so be patient and maintain a consistent presence.

Writing Effective Press Releases

Press releases are an essential tool for generating media attention and getting your brand in front of a broader audience. A well-written press release follows a specific format and includes all the essential information needed to cover a story. This includes a headline, sub headline, opening paragraph, background information, and quotes. A good press release should be concise and focused on one specific message or announcement.

When crafting your press release, put yourself in the shoes of a journalist who is receiving your pitch. Ask yourself whether your story is newsworthy, and if it aligns with the interests of the particular media outlet you are targeting. Be sure to include all the necessary contact information so that journalists can reach you easily.

Pitching Stories and Ideas to the Media

Pitching stories and ideas to the media is the process of presenting a story idea or angle to a journalist or editor in the hopes of securing coverage. A well-crafted pitch should be tailored to the specific publication and journalist you are reaching out to. When pitching, be sure to highlight the most important and unique aspects of your story, and demonstrate why it is relevant to their audience.

When following up on a pitch, be mindful of the journalist's schedule and deadlines. If you have not received a response after a few days, follow up with a polite email or phone call. While it is important to be persistent, it is equally important to respect the journalist's decision if they choose not to cover your story.

Leveraging Social Media for PR Success

Social media can play a critical role in a PR strategy, allowing businesses to engage with the public in real-time and share information with a broader audience. When using social media for PR, it is important to maintain a consistent brand voice, craft messaging that resonates with your target audience, and stay up-to-date with social media trends and algorithms.

To leverage social media for PR, start by developing a social content calendar that aligns with your overall PR strategy. The content you share should be tailored to your target audience and should aim to establish your brand as a thought leader in your industry. Engage with your followers and respond to their comments and feedback, and when appropriate, use social media to amplify your messages and announcements.

Monitoring and Managing Online Reputation

In today's digital age, managing your online reputation is more important than ever. A single negative review or social media post can have a significant impact on your brand image and can lead to lost business. To safeguard your online reputation, it is important to monitor mentions of your brand online and respond quickly to any negative comments or reviews.

When managing your online reputation, it is important to be transparent and honest in your responses. If you make a mistake, acknowledge it, and take responsibility for your actions. Be sincere in your apologies and offer solutions to resolve the issue. By remaining proactive and responsive, you can maintain a positive image and protect your brand reputation.

Measuring the Success of PR Efforts

Measuring the success of your PR efforts is critical to understanding the value of your investments and to optimizing future campaigns. Key metrics to measure PR success include media coverage, impression reach, website traffic, and social media engagement. While it can be difficult to quantitatively measure the impact of PR, investing in data and analytics tools can help to provide useful insights.

To measure the success of your PR efforts, start by setting clear objectives and tracking metrics that align with those objectives. Continuously monitor and analyze your PR campaign across all channels, and use the data to inform future efforts. Be prepared to adjust your strategy based on the results of your analysis.

Avoiding Common PR Mistakes

One of the most common mistakes businesses make when it comes to PR is focusing too much on promoting products or services, and not enough on building relationships with the media and public. It is important to prioritize relationship building and always be mindful of your audience's interests. Additionally, failing to invest in the right tools and training can also lead to suboptimal results. To avoid these mistakes, invest in a high-quality PR team or agency, allocate sufficient time and resources to your PR campaigns, and continuously focus on building and maintaining strong relationships with journalists and the media.

In conclusion, effective public relations is critical for establishing your brand's image, building credibility, and connecting with your target audience. It requires clear objectives, tailored messaging, relationship-building, effective media outreach, and continuous measurement and analysis. By investing in a comprehensive PR strategy and consistently applying best practices, businesses can successfully manage their reputation, cultivate valuable relationships, and achieve long-term marketing success.

CHAPTER 9: INFLUENCER MARKETING FOR MAXIMUM IMPACT

Influencer marketing has become an increasingly popular tactic in recent years, and for good reason. By partnering with influential individuals in your industry, you can tap into their existing audience and leverage their credibility to increase brand awareness and drive sales. In this chapter, we will explore best practices for implementing an effective influencer marketing strategy.

Identifying Relevant Influencers

The first step in implementing an effective influencer marketing strategy is identifying relevant influencers in your industry. This requires a deep understanding of your target audience and the individuals they look up to and trust. Start by researching individuals who are active on social media platforms and blogs that are relevant to your industry. Look for individuals who have a large following and a high level of engagement with their audience.

Once you have identified potential influencers, take time to review their content and assess whether or not they are a good fit for your brand. Look for individuals who are aligned with your values and mission and who have a genuine interest in your brand and products.

Building Relationships with Influencers

Building relationships with influencers is a critical step in successful influencer marketing. Without a strong relationship based on mutual trust and respect, it can be difficult to achieve your desired outcome. One effective way to build relationships with influencers is to start by engaging with their content. Comment on their posts, share their content, and show genuine interest in what they are doing.

Another effective strategy for building relationships with influencers is to offer value. Consider how you can help the influencer and their audience. Perhaps you can provide them with exclusive access to your products or services, or offer to collaborate on content. By providing value, you can demonstrate your willingness to establish a mutually beneficial relationship.

Collaborating with Influencers on Content and Campaigns

Collaborating with influencers on content and campaigns is a great way to leverage their existing audience for your brand. Many influencers have a large and engaged following, and by partnering with them, you can tap into their credibility and reach.

When collaborating with influencers, it's important to have a clear and specific goal in mind. This could include increasing brand awareness, driving sales, or launching a new product or service. Develop a clear and concise brief that outlines your expectations and desired outcome.

In addition, make sure to give the influencer creative freedom to develop content in a way that feels authentic and aligned with their brand. Provide guidance and input, but be willing to trust the influencer's expertise and knowledge of their audience.

Measuring the Success of Influencer Marketing Efforts

Measuring the success of influencer marketing can be challenging, but it is critical to determine whether or not your efforts are having an impact. Some key metrics to monitor include engagement rates, follower growth, website traffic, and sales. It's also important to establish a clear benchmark for success and track your progress over time.

One effective strategy for measuring the success of influencer marketing efforts is to establish unique tracking links or discount codes that are only available to the influencer's audience. This makes it easy to track clicks and sales from the influencer's promotion.

Staying Up-to-Date with Changes in Influencer Marketing Trends

Influencer marketing is a rapidly evolving field, and it's important to stay up-to-date with changes in trends and best practices. As social media platforms continue to evolve and new influencers emerge, it's critical to adjust your strategy to keep up with the changes.

One emerging trend in influencer marketing is the use of micro-influencers. These are individuals who have a smaller following but a highly engaged audience. By partnering with micro-influencers, you can tap into a highly targeted audience and increase the likelihood of conversion.

Another trend in influencer marketing is the use of user-generated content. By encouraging your customers to share their experiences with your product or service, you can leverage their credibility and reach to increase brand awareness.

Avoiding Common Influencer Marketing Mistakes

While influencer marketing can be a highly effective marketing strategy, there are also several common mistakes to avoid. Perhaps the biggest mistake is failing to establish a genuine and authentic relationship with the influencer. This can lead to a lack of trust and a failure to achieve the desired outcome.

Another common mistake is failing to establish clear goals and metrics for success. Without a clear understanding of what you want to achieve, it can be difficult to measure the success of your efforts.

Finally, it's important to avoid partnering with influencers simply based on their follower count. While a large following may seem impressive, it's the quality of the engagement and alignment with your brand that ultimately matters.

Conclusion

Influencer marketing can be a highly effective strategy for increasing brand awareness and driving sales. By identifying relevant influencers, building relationships with them, and collaborating on campaigns, you can tap into their credibility and reach. As with any marketing strategy, it's important to measure the success of your efforts and stay up-to-date with changes in trends and best practices. By avoiding common mistakes and continually innovating, you can achieve long-term marketing success through influencer marketing.

CHAPTER 10: EVENT MARKETING FOR BUSINESS SUCCESS

In today's digital age, it's easy to forget the power of an in-person event. However, event marketing remains one of the most effective ways to connect with your target audience and build brand awareness. From trade shows to product launches, events offer a unique opportunity to engage with potential customers and showcase your brand's personality.

Planning and executing a successful event, however, takes careful planning and attention to detail. In this chapter, we'll explore the key steps involved in event marketing and provide tips for making your next event both impactful and profitable.

1. Choosing the Right Type of Event

The first step in planning an event is to choose the right type of event for your business. Consider your target audience and your overall marketing strategy. Do you want to host a conference or trade show to educate potential customers about your industry? Or do you want to host a product launch or experiential event to generate buzz and excitement around a new product?

Be realistic about your budget and resources when planning your event. A trade show or conference may require a significant investment, but can be a powerful lead generation tool. On the other hand, a smaller, more intimate event like a dinner party or influencer event may be more cost-effective and yield a higher return on investment.

2. Developing a Targeted Guest List

Once you've chosen the type of event you want to host, it's time to develop a targeted guest list. Who do you want to attend your event? Consider your buyer persona and create a list of potential attendees who fit that profile. Consider inviting key industry influencers, members of the media, and other thought leaders who can help spread the word about your event.

It's important to approach your guest list strategically and not simply invite as many people as possible. Look for opportunities to build relationships with potential customers and create a positive, memorable experience that leaves a lasting impression.

3. Creating Engaging Event Content and Activities

The content and activities you offer at your event can make or break the experience for attendees. Consider what types of activities and experiences will resonate most with your target audience. Will they enjoy a keynote speaker or panel discussion? Or would they prefer interactive, hands-on experiences like product demos or workshops?

The key is to offer a mix of activities that appeal to different preferences and learning styles. Consider offering multiple tracks or sessions so attendees can customize their experience. Don't forget to incorporate opportunities for networking and building relationships with other attendees and industry professionals.

4. Promoting Events Effectively

Effective promotion is key to the success of any event. Utilize a mix of channels to get the word out and reach your target audience. Consider using email marketing to promote the event to your existing customer base, social media to reach a wider audience, and targeted advertising to drive registrations.

It's also important to create a sense of urgency and excitement around the event. Offer special early bird pricing or perks for registering early, and create visually appealing promotional materials that amplify the experience attendees can expect to have.

5. Measuring the Success of Events

Measuring the success of your event is critical to understanding how effective your marketing efforts have been. Be sure to establish key performance indicators (KPIs) before the event, such as the number of registrations, leads generated, and social media mentions.

During the event, track attendee engagement and feedback to identify areas for improvement and capture potential testimonials or case studies. After the event, analyze your results and compare against your KPIs to determine the ROI of your event marketing efforts.

6. Leveraging Technology for Event Marketing

Technology can be a game-changer when it comes to event marketing. From event software and mobile apps to augmented reality and virtual reality experiences, there are endless opportunities to use technology to enhance the attendee experience and create buzz around your event.

Consider partnering with technology providers or start-ups to create unique experiences that set your event apart from the competition. Utilize data and analytics tools to track attendee engagement and personalize the event experience based on individual preferences.

MARKETING SUCCESS SECRETS

7. Avoiding Common Event Marketing Mistakes

Effective event marketing requires attention to detail and careful planning. Common mistakes to avoid include failing to establish clear goals, underestimating the importance of a targeted guest list, or overlooking key event logistics like transportation, accommodations, and catering.

It's also important to have a clear emergency plan in place in case of unexpected issues like inclement weather or a power outage. By being proactive and planning for potential challenges, you can avoid common pitfalls and create a successful, impactful event.

In conclusion, event marketing remains one of the most effective ways to connect with your target audience and build brand awareness. By following these key steps and avoiding common mistakes, you can plan and execute a successful event and take your marketing efforts to the next level.

CHAPTER 11: MOBILE MARKETING FOR MAXIMUM IMPACT

In today's world, mobile phones are an integral part of our lives. Everyone has a smartphone, and we spend hours scrolling through social media, watching videos, and reading emails. Therefore, it is an absolute necessity for businesses to develop a mobile marketing strategy to reach their target audience effectively. In this chapter, we will explore the benefits of a mobile marketing strategy, various tactics for executing it, and mistakes to avoid.

Understanding the Importance of Mobile Marketing:

Mobile marketing is crucial because it enables businesses to connect with their target audience where they are most active - on their phones. According to a study conducted by Pew Research, 96% of Americans own a mobile phone, out of which 81% are smartphones. Additionally, 90% of the time spent on a smartphone is spent on mobile apps. Therefore, mobile marketing can provide businesses with a direct line of communication with their target audience.

Developing a Mobile Marketing Strategy:

❖   Develop a responsive website: A responsive website

is a website that is built to provide an optimal viewing experience on mobile devices. Therefore, it is important to design a website that can be easily navigated on a mobile device. You can also take advantage of Google's mobile-friendly test tool to ensure your website is mobile-friendly.

❖ Optimize email marketing for mobile: As per the stats, more than 50% of emails are opened on mobile devices. Therefore, it is essential to create mobile-friendly emails. Create emails with a responsive design, optimally sized images, and easy-to-tap links.

❖ Utilize SMS and MMS messaging: SMS and MMS marketing can be an effective way to reach customers with time-sensitive information, offers, and coupons. You can also use SMS and MMS messaging to gather customer feedback and conduct surveys.

❖ Build your own mobile app: Building an app provides you with an opportunity to engage with your customers in a unique way. An app can provide customers with quick access to your products or services, enable them to make purchases, and receive personalized offers.

❖ Leverage location-based marketing: Location-based marketing allows you to create personalized marketing campaigns based on your customer's location. Geo-targeted ads can provide you with valuable insights about customer behavior, foot traffic, and sales.

Mobile Marketing Tactics:

❖ SMS Campaigns: Short message service (SMS) campaigns are a way of reaching your customers with a short and concise message. SMSes can be used to keep your customers informed about your products, promotions, offers, and deals. But, remember to be relevant and avoid spamming.

❖ In-App Advertising: In-app advertising provides you with a platform to advertise directly to your target audience through various apps. You can take advantage of apps that are relevant to your product or service and create advertisements that resonate with your target audience.

❖ Social Media Advertising: Social media platforms like Facebook, Twitter, and Instagram offer various advertising options that provide businesses with an opportunity to reach their target audience effectively. You can create mobile-optimized ads that are specifically targeted towards mobile users.

❖ QR Codes: Quick Response (QR) codes can be used to promote your products and services by directing customers to your website or social media pages. A QR code can be scanned using a smartphone camera or a QR code reader, and it will direct the user to the website or social media page linked to the code.

❖ Mobile-optimized Content: Mobile users prefer content that is quick, concise, and easily consumable. Therefore, it is important to create mobile-optimized content that can be enjoyed on-the-go. Use short paragraphs, bullet points, easy-to-read fonts, and engaging visuals.

Mistakes to Avoid:

❖ Not having a mobile-friendly website: If your website is not mobile-friendly, you risk losing customers who are browsing on their mobile devices.

❖ Not optimizing your emails and newsletters for mobile: If your email isn't optimized for mobile, there is a chance the recipient may delete it or not engage with it.

❖ Neglecting location-based advertising: Not leveraging the power of location-based advertising can make your marketing campaigns less effective.

❖   Not understanding your audience's mobile behavior: Understanding how your audience interacts with their mobile devices is critical for developing an effective mobile marketing strategy.

In conclusion, a mobile marketing strategy is essential for businesses that wish to stay ahead of the competition. By understanding how your audience interacts with mobile devices, you can develop effective strategies that will help you reach your target audience where they are most active. Remember to stay up-to-date with changes in mobile marketing trends, continuously innovate and avoid common mistakes.

CHAPTER 12: VIDEO MARKETING FOR BUSINESS SUCCESS

In today's fast-paced digital age, creating high-quality video content is a critical component of any successful marketing strategy. Video marketing offers businesses the opportunity to connect with their audience on a deeper level, while also delivering engaging and informative content that drives conversions.

Understanding the Importance of Video Marketing

Video marketing is an essential part of any modern marketing strategy. With the rise of video-sharing platforms such as YouTube, Vimeo, and Facebook, it has become easier than ever to create and share video content with a global audience. Additionally, video content is more engaging and memorable than other forms of content, making it an ideal way to educate and inform potential customers.

One of the most significant advantages of video marketing is its ability to capture attention quickly. As people have shorter attention spans today than ever before, it's more important than ever to make a strong first impression. Video content can do just that by grabbing your audience's attention and holding it long enough for them to absorb your message.

Crafting a Video Marketing Strategy

To maximize the benefits of video marketing, businesses need to create a video marketing strategy that aligns with their overall marketing objectives. This requires a deep understanding of the target audience and the types of videos that are most likely to resonate with them.

When developing a video marketing strategy, it's important to identify the various types of videos that will be produced. This could include product demos, company culture videos, customer testimonials, industry news, training videos, and much more. Determining the right mix of videos depends on the nature of your business and the preferences of your target audience.

Creating High-Quality Video Content

Creating high-quality video content requires careful planning and execution. This requires attention to every aspect of the video production process, including scriptwriting, casting, filming, editing, and post-production. By working with a professional video production company, businesses can ensure that their video content is of the highest quality and will stand out in a crowded marketplace.

When creating video content, businesses should also consider the importance of optimizing videos for search engines. This requires a thorough understanding of search engine optimization (SEO) best practices, including keyword research, video tags, and descriptions. By optimizing videos for search engines, businesses can increase their visibility and attract more traffic to their website.

Leveraging Video Across All Marketing Channels

To maximize the impact of video content, businesses should

leverage it across all their marketing channels. This could include embedding videos on websites, sharing videos on social media, incorporating videos into email marketing campaigns, and using videos in paid advertising campaigns.

When incorporating video content into marketing campaigns, it's important to tailor the videos to the specific platform being used. This means optimizing the length and format of the videos to suit each platform and its audience.

Measuring the Success of Video Marketing Efforts

As with any marketing strategy, it's important to measure the success of video marketing efforts. This requires a thorough understanding of key performance indicators (KPIs), including video views, engagement metrics, click-through rates (CTR), and conversions.

By analyzing these metrics, businesses can identify which videos are most effective in driving engagement and conversions. This can then be used to optimize future video content and improve overall marketing performance.

Staying Up-to-Date with Changes in Video Marketing Trends

As the video marketing landscape continues to evolve, it's important for businesses to stay up-to-date with changes in video marketing trends. This means understanding emerging video formats, such as vertical videos and live streaming, and incorporating them into marketing strategies.

It also means following the latest advancements in video production technology, such as virtual reality and 360-degree video, and exploring their potential applications in marketing campaigns.

Avoiding Common Video Marketing Mistakes

To maximize the benefits of video marketing, it's important to avoid common mistakes that can hamper its effectiveness. This includes failing to optimize videos for search engines, neglecting to tailor videos to individual platforms, and failing to measure the success of video marketing efforts.

It's also important to avoid producing videos that are overly promotional or lacking in substance. Instead, video content should be informative, engaging, and focused on delivering value to the viewer.

Conclusion

Video marketing is a critical component of any modern marketing strategy. By crafting high-quality video content that resonates with the target audience and leveraging it across all marketing channels, businesses can improve their overall marketing performance and drive meaningful conversions. Staying up-to-date with changes in video marketing trends and avoiding common mistakes is essential to maximizing the effectiveness of video marketing efforts.

CHAPTER 13: AFFILIATE MARKETING FOR MAXIMUM IMPACT

Affiliate marketing is a type of performance-based marketing in which a business rewards affiliates for each visitor or customer brought about by the affiliate's own marketing efforts. Affiliate marketing has become a popular method of increasing online sales for businesses of all sizes and is an essential part of a successful digital marketing strategy. In this chapter, we'll explore the fundamentals of affiliate marketing, how to choose the right affiliate program, recruit and manage affiliates, create effective affiliate marketing campaigns, and avoid common affiliate marketing mistakes.

Understanding the Fundamentals of Affiliate Marketing

Affiliate marketing is a form of advertising in which businesses pay affiliates to promote their products or services to their own audiences. Affiliates are rewarded for each visitor or customer they refer to the business through their own unique affiliate link or code. Affiliate marketing is a mutually beneficial arrangement for both the business and the affiliate. The business gains exposure to a new audience, and the affiliate earns a commission for promoting the business's products or services.

Affiliate marketing can be an effective way for businesses to increase their online sales, boost their brand awareness, and build relationships with new audiences. For affiliates, it can be a lucrative way to earn extra income by promoting products or services they genuinely believe in to their own followers.

Choosing the Right Affiliate Program for Your Business

Choosing the right affiliate program is an essential step in creating a successful affiliate marketing campaign. When choosing an affiliate program, it's important to consider the following factors:

❖   The commission rate: The commission rate is the percentage of each sale that the affiliate will earn as a commission. It's important to choose an affiliate program that offers a competitive commission rate that will attract quality affiliates.

❖ The product or service: The product or service being offered by the business should be something that the affiliate is genuinely interested in and believes in. It's important to choose a product or service that fits in with the affiliate's brand and target audience.

❖   The affiliate tracking and reporting system: A good affiliate program should offer an easy-to-use tracking and reporting system that allows affiliates to track their sales and commissions accurately.

❖   The payment schedule: The payment schedule is the frequency with which the affiliate will be paid. It's important to choose an affiliate program that offers a payment schedule that is fair and timely.

Recruiting and Managing Affiliates

Once you have chosen the right affiliate program for your business, the next step is to recruit and manage affiliates.

When recruiting affiliates, it's important to focus on quality over quantity. It's better to have a few high-quality affiliates than a large number of low-quality affiliates.

To attract quality affiliates, it's important to provide them with high-quality marketing materials that they can use to promote your products or services. This could include product images, videos, and text descriptions.

It's also important to communicate regularly with your affiliates and provide them with support and guidance to help them succeed. This could include providing them with tips on how to promote your products or services effectively and offering them incentives for achieving certain sales targets.

Creating effective affiliate marketing campaigns

Creating effective affiliate marketing campaigns is all about providing affiliates with the tools and support they need to promote your products or services effectively. This could include providing them with unique affiliate links, offering them exclusive promotions and discounts, and creating engaging marketing materials that they can share with their own audiences.

It's also important to track and analyze the performance of your affiliate marketing campaigns regularly. This will help you to identify which campaigns are working well and which ones need to be improved.

Maximizing ROI through affiliate marketing

Affiliate marketing can be an effective way for businesses to maximize their ROI by generating more sales and exposure through the promotion of their products or services by affiliates. By choosing the right affiliate program, recruiting and managing high-quality affiliates, creating engaging marketing campaigns, and tracking and analyzing performance regularly, businesses can ensure that their affiliate marketing efforts are successful.

Avoiding common affiliate marketing mistakes

Like any marketing strategy, affiliate marketing is not without its pitfalls. Some common mistakes to avoid include:

❖ Choosing low-quality affiliates: It's important to focus on quality over quantity when choosing affiliates. Choosing low-quality affiliates can damage your brand reputation and lead to poor sales performance.

❖ Offering low commission rates: Low commission rates can discourage high-quality affiliates from promoting your products or services. It's important to offer a competitive commission rate that will attract quality affiliates.

❖ Failing to track performance: Failing to track the performance of your affiliate marketing campaigns can lead to poor performance and wasted resources. It's important to track and analyze the performance of your campaigns regularly to ensure that they are effective.

Conclusion

Affiliate marketing can be an effective way for businesses to increase their online sales, boost their brand awareness, and build relationships with new audiences. By choosing the right affiliate program, recruiting and managing high-quality affiliates, creating engaging marketing campaigns, and tracking and analyzing performance regularly, businesses can ensure that their affiliate marketing efforts are successful. However, it's important to avoid common affiliate marketing mistakes such as choosing low-quality affiliates, offering low commission rates, and failing to track performance. With the right approach, affiliate marketing can be an essential part of a successful digital marketing strategy.

CHAPTER 14: PODCAST MARKETING FOR BUSINESS SUCCESS

Podcast marketing has been growing in popularity over recent years, and for good reason. With millions of people tuning in to podcasts every day, this platform presents an opportunity for businesses to reach a new and engaged audience. In this chapter, we will explore the importance of podcast marketing for businesses and outline some key strategies for creating a successful podcast.

Understanding the Importance of Podcast Marketing

Podcasting has rapidly become one of the most valuable platforms for businesses to connect with their audience. Podcasts are a great way to create original content, build deeper relationships with customers, and generate more leads and sales.

One of the key benefits of podcast marketing is the ability to create a loyal audience. Unlike social media where you're competing for attention in a sea of endless distractions, podcasts are an intimate platform that allows you to build a personal connection with your listeners. By regularly producing quality content, you can develop a devoted group of fans that tune in week after week.

Additionally, podcasts also allow you to showcase your expertise, build your brand's visibility, and share your message with a new audience. As people tune in to your podcast, they become more familiar with your brand and the offerings you have, and they are more likely to make a purchase or engage with your brand in the future.

Creating and Promoting a Podcast for your Business

Before you jump into podcast marketing, there are a few things you should consider. Namely, what your podcast will be about, and who your target audience is.

To create a podcast that resonates with your audience, you need to cover topics that are relevant and valuable to them. A good way to start is to identify the pain points or questions that your target audience has and to create episodes that offer solutions. For example, if you run a fitness business, you could create a podcast about healthy eating, or workout routines.

Once you have defined your podcast topic, it's time to start recording. If you're new to podcasting, you'll need to invest in some basic equipment, like a microphone and recording software. Start by creating a few practice episodes to find your footing; then, once you're comfortable, you can start publishing on a regular schedule.

Promoting your podcast is just as important as creating one. You need to make sure that your podcast reaches your target audience and gains traction. First, optimize your podcast by creating compelling titles and descriptions to attract listeners. Then, share your podcast on social media and other relevant networks. Identify social media influencers in your niche and ask them to promote your podcast to their audience. Additionally, don't forget to integrate your podcast with your other marketing channels by mentioning it on your website, email marketing campaigns, and other digital marketing platforms.

Developing Engaging Podcast Content

The key to creating a successful podcast is to produce engaging and high-quality content. Your content should be informative, unique, and above all else, entertaining. Focus on creating stories or infusing humor into your podcast episodes to keep listeners engaged and entertained.

Another important aspect of your podcast is audio quality. Make sure that you invest in a quality microphone and audio editing software to make your podcast sound as professional as possible. If your podcast audio quality is poor, people will switch off, no matter how great your content may be.

Building a Loyal Podcast Audience

Marketing your podcast is essential in building a loyal audience. One of the most important things you can do to ensure the success of your podcast is to consistently produce high-quality content. By creating a regular publishing schedule, listeners will come to expect new episodes, and your podcast can become a part of their regular routine.

Engaging with your listeners is another essential aspect of building a loyal podcast audience. Respond to comments and questions on your podcast's social media handles and always seek feedback from your listeners. You can also encourage listeners to leave reviews on popular podcast platforms like iTunes or Google Play.

Optimizing Podcasts for Search Engines

SEO is just as important in podcasts as it is on your website. To increase the visibility of your podcast, choose episode titles, descriptions, and show notes with relevant keywords. This will help your podcast become more discoverable on search engines.

Additionally, you can optimize your podcast for search engines by including relevant links within your show notes that direct listeners to other pages on your website. This can help increase the overall traffic to your website and drive more conversions.

Measuring the Success of Podcast Marketing Efforts

Podcast analytics allow you to track your podcast's performance and determine whether you're reaching your targeted audience. You can assess the success of your podcast through various metrics like total downloads, audience engagement, and the number of shares on social media.

By monitoring your podcast analytics, you can better understand what topics and episodes resonate with your audience and adapt accordingly. You can also get feedback from listeners on what topics they would like to hear about in future episodes.

Staying Up-to-date with Changes in Podcast Marketing Trends

Podcast marketing is constantly evolving, and it's essential to stay up-to-date with the latest trends and best practices. Be sure to keep an eye on how other businesses in your niche are using podcasting, and always be open to learning from the successes and failures of others in the industry.

Avoiding Common Podcast Marketing Mistakes

One of the most common podcast marketing mistakes is failing to produce quality content consistently. By committing to a regular publishing schedule, you can create a sense of anticipation for new episodes and build a loyal following.

Another mistake is neglecting social media promotion. Promoting your podcast on social media is essential for getting the word out and building a following. It's also important to monitor listener feedback and use it to improve your content and overall podcast experience.

Conclusion

Podcast marketing is an incredibly powerful tool for businesses to connect with their audience and build a loyal following. By carefully crafting engaging content, optimizing your podcast for search engines, and monitoring analytics, you can create a thriving podcast that grows your business. Remember that like any marketing channel, consistency and creativity are the keys to success. So don't be afraid to incorporate podcast marketing into your overall marketing strategy and experiment with new formats and topics along the way.

CHAPTER 15: BRAND PARTNERSHIPS FOR MAXIMUM IMPACT

In today's highly competitive business landscape, it is essential for companies to find ways to stand out and build their brand. One effective strategy for achieving this is brand partnerships. By collaborating with other brands in complementary industries, businesses can expand their reach, gain exposure to new audiences, and ultimately increase their bottom line.

Identifying Relevant Brand Partnerships

The first step in creating successful brand partnerships is identifying those that are most relevant to your business. This requires a thorough understanding of your target audience and their interests, as well as an awareness of the broader market trends and developments.

For example, a company that produces high-quality organic food products may consider partnering with a health and wellness brand to promote a healthy lifestyle. Similarly, a technology company producing innovative products for the fitness industry may want to partner with a prominent fitness brand to tap into their established customer base.

When looking for potential brand partnerships, it is important to consider the values, image, and personality of the partner brand.

It is essential to ensure that both brands are aligned in terms of vision and goals, and that the partnership will be a good fit for both parties.

Leveraging Brand Partnerships for Increased Visibility

Once you have identified potential brand partnerships, the next step is to leverage these partnerships for maximum impact. One way to do this is to collaborate on content and campaigns that showcase both brands.

For example, a partnership between a fashion brand and a sports brand may result in a joint marketing campaign that features athletes wearing the fashion brand's clothing while engaging in sports activities. This campaign not only showcases the fashion brand's products but also emphasizes the connection between the two brands and their shared values.

Collaborating on content and campaigns can also include joint product releases, social media campaigns, and events. These partnerships help to increase visibility and exposure to new audiences, generating buzz and excitement around both brands.

Measuring the Success of Brand Partnership Efforts

As with any marketing effort, it is essential to measure the success of brand partnerships to ensure that they are delivering the desired results. This requires setting clear objectives and KPIs before entering into the partnership and regularly monitoring progress against these goals.

Some common KPIs for brand partnerships may include increases in website traffic, social media engagement, and sales conversions. Measuring the success of brand partnerships may also involve gathering feedback from customers and tracking brand sentiment.

Staying Up-to-Date with Changes in Brand Partnership Trends

Brand partnerships continue to evolve and adapt to changes in the market and emerging trends. As such, it is essential for businesses to stay up-to-date with these changing trends to ensure that their partnerships remain relevant and impactful.

For example, an emerging trend in brand partnerships is the rise of cause marketing, where brands partner with non-profit organizations or charities to promote social responsibility and sustainability. Another trend is the rise of partnerships between brands and influencers, who can help to promote the brand's message and expand its reach to new audiences.

Maximizing ROI through Brand Partnerships

Brand partnerships have the potential to expand the reach and exposure of a business, increase its visibility, and ultimately drive sales and revenue growth. However, it is essential to carefully select the right partner and carefully plan and execute the partnership to maximize ROI.

To achieve maximum impact, businesses should focus on creating partnerships that are aligned with their core values and that help to differentiate them from the competition. They should track and measure the success of their partnerships, gathering data and insights that can be used to optimize future partnerships.

Avoiding Common Brand Partnership Mistakes

While brand partnerships can be highly effective, there are also common mistakes that businesses should avoid when pursuing them. These include partnering with a brand that is not aligned with their vision or values, failing to clearly define objectives and expected outcomes, and not investing sufficient resources in the partnership.

Another common mistake is failing to adequately protect your brand's intellectual property, such as names, logos, and trademarks, when entering into a partnership. This can lead to legal disputes and damage to your brand's reputation.

Building Long-Term Brand Partnerships for Sustained Success

To achieve sustained success through brand partnerships, it is essential to build long-term relationships with partner brands. This requires regular communication, collaboration, and a commitment to shared goals and values.

By building long-term partnerships, businesses can leverage the strengths and assets of both brands to generate significant benefits and create a competitive advantage in the market. It also allows them to stay ahead of emerging trends and changes in the market, adapting their approach and strategies to remain relevant and impactful.

CHAPTER 16: CUSTOMER RELATIONSHIP MANAGEMENT (CRM) FOR BUSINESS SUCCESS

Every business wants to keep their customers happy, but how do you ensure that they remain satisfied and loyal in the long term? One of the key strategies is to implement a Customer Relationship Management (CRM) system that allows you to manage and track interactions with your customers. CRM systems offer a range of benefits, from capturing customer data to creating targeted marketing campaigns, and they can play a crucial role in driving business success.

Understanding the Importance of CRM

At its simplest, CRM is about creating better relationships with your customers. It involves collecting and analyzing data about customer behavior and preferences, which can then be used to provide a more personalized and relevant experience. By better understanding your customers, you can tailor your products and services to meet their needs, and build lasting relationships that lead to loyalty and advocacy.

Choosing the Right CRM System

There are dozens of CRM systems on the market, ranging from basic contact management tools to more complex solutions that offer features like marketing automation and analytics. Choosing the right system for your business requires a clear understanding of your needs and goals, as well as a consideration of budget and scalability.

Capture and Manage Customer Data

The first step in any CRM system is to capture and manage customer data. This can include basic information like names and email addresses, as well as more detailed data like purchase history, website interactions, and social media activity. A good CRM system should allow you to capture this data automatically, and also provide tools for manual data entry if necessary.

Build Customer Profiles and Personas

Once you have captured customer data, you can use it to build profiles and personas that represent different segments of your customer base. This involves identifying patterns and trends in customer behavior, preferences, and demographics, and using that information to create detailed profiles of your ideal customers. Personas can be used to tailor marketing messages, create targeted campaigns, and even develop new products and services.

Develop Effective Email Marketing Campaigns

Email marketing is one of the most effective forms of marketing, and a good CRM system can make it even more powerful. By segmenting your email list based on customer profiles, you can create highly targeted campaigns that are more likely to resonate with your audience. Personalization is key here, as customers are more likely to engage with content that is tailored to their specific needs and interests.

Utilize Segmentation and Personalization in CRM

Segmentation and personalization are two of the most important aspects of CRM, and they should be integrated into every aspect of your customer interactions. By segmenting your customer base, you can create personalized messages and experiences that are tailored to individual needs and preferences. Personalization can include everything from email greetings to product recommendations, and it can make a huge difference in customer satisfaction and loyalty.

Measuring the Success of CRM Efforts

Like any marketing strategy, CRM requires ongoing measurement and analysis to determine its effectiveness. This can involve tracking customer engagement metrics like open rates, clicks, and conversions, as well as more qualitative data like customer satisfaction and loyalty. By regularly analyzing this data, you can identify areas where your CRM strategy is working well, as well as areas that need improvement.

Avoiding Common CRM Mistakes

Finally, it is important to avoid common mistakes that can derail your CRM efforts. These can include everything from failing to capture accurate customer data to over-personalizing marketing messages. Other common mistakes include failing to segment your customer base effectively, or using spammy or irrelevant marketing tactics that turn off customers. To avoid these pitfalls, it is important to stay up-to-date with best practices and trends in CRM, and to regularly audit your processes and strategies to ensure they are delivering the desired results.

CHAPTER 17: E-COMMERCE STRATEGIES FOR MAXIMUM IMPACT

With the growth of the internet and the digitization of business transactions, more and more businesses are opting to set up online stores, and for good reasons. E-commerce provides businesses with access to a wider audience, reduces overhead costs associated with traditional brick-and-mortar stores, and offers customers with a more convenient shopping experience.

However, setting up an e-commerce store is not enough to guarantee success. In this chapter, we will explore the fundamentals of e-commerce as well as some strategies that companies can employ to maximize their online sales.

Understanding the fundamentals of e-commerce

Before diving into the strategies, it is crucial for businesses to comprehend the essentials of e-commerce. The following are some of the basic concepts that businesses need to understand when setting up an online store.

❖ User Interface Design: The user interface is the environment that customers interact with when visiting an online store. A well-designed user interface that is user-friendly, responsive, and visually appealing can increase the chances of customers making a purchase.

❖ Payment Gateways: Payment gateways facilitate secure online transactions by transferring money from the customer's account to the seller's account. A reliable payment gateway is essential for customer trust and retention.

❖ Shipping and Logistics: Shipping and logistics involve safely delivering the product from the seller's warehouse to the customer's doorstep. Smooth logistics and efficient shipping operations are vital to any e-commerce store's success.

Maximizing online sales

Now that we understand the fundamentals let's dive into the strategies that businesses can employ to maximize their online sales.

❖ Optimize Landing Pages: A landing page is the first page that a customer sees when they click on your advertisement or product link. A well-optimized landing page should be relevant to the advertisement that brought the customer there and should include a clear call-to-action (CTA).

❖ Cross-Selling and Upselling: Cross-selling involves suggesting similar or complementary products to the customer, while upselling entails encouraging the customer to purchase a higher-priced item with added benefits. Cross-selling and upselling can boost revenue and customer retention.

❖ Enhance Product Pages: A well-crafted product page can significantly increase the chances of customers making a purchase. Key features on a product page should include high-quality images, detailed product descriptions, customer reviews, and social proof, among others.

❖ Leverage Email Marketing: Email marketing is an effective tool for keeping customers engaged and informed about new products, promotions, and offers through newsletters and personalized emails.

❖ Retargeting Ads: Retargeting ads refer to advertisements that target customers who have previously visited your online store. These ads can entice them to return and complete their previous purchase or make a new one.

❖ Simplify Checkout Process: A complex checkout process can result in cart abandonment. To avoid this, businesses should streamline the checkout process by minimizing the number of steps, offering various payment options, and focusing on mobile optimization.

❖ Social Media Marketing: An active social media presence allows businesses to interact with customers and promote their products. A social media platform such as Instagram can also serve as an additional sales channel by incorporating a shoppable post feature.

Conclusion

E-commerce has revolutionized the way businesses conduct transactions. The success of e-commerce largely depends on the effectiveness of the strategies employed. By incorporating these strategies and continually adapting to changing customer needs and market trends, businesses can maximize their online sales and stay ahead of the competition.

CHAPTER 18: CUSTOMER SERVICE FOR BUSINESS SUCCESS

Customers are the cornerstone of any business, and providing excellent customer service is essential to create a loyal customer base. In today's fast-paced and ever-changing business world, customer service is no longer limited to the traditional methods of phone calls and emails. The rise of social media has made it more important than ever to provide excellent customer service, as unhappy customers are more likely to share their negative experiences online.

Understanding the Importance of Customer Service

Customer service is the backbone of any business, and it is essential to prioritize it from the outset. Good customer service is about creating a positive brand experience for your customers. Customers who have a positive experience are more likely to become repeat customers, and they are also more likely to recommend you to their friends and family.

Developing a Customer Service Strategy

Developing a customer service strategy involves setting

guidelines on how you plan to interact and engage with your customers. Some starting points might include the types of channels you prefer to communicate through (email, phone, social media), typical response time, and how you plan to address negative feedback.

Building a Customer Service Team

A customer service team should be made up of people who are enthusiastic, proactive, and are passionate about making sure the customer's voice is heard. A customer service representative should have empathy skills because they need to be able to put themselves in the customer's shoes to understand where they are coming from.

Providing Effective Customer Support Across all Channels

One of the most critical aspects of customer service is how you communicate with your customers. Today, businesses need to be communicative across all platforms to build a robust customer service experience. This includes answering questions via Facebook Messenger, backing up your claims on Instagram, responding to Google reviews, and handling customer service requests through email, phone, or text message.

Leveraging Technology for Customer Service Success

The rise of technology has significantly impacted customer service. Customer relationship management systems (CRMs) are now commonplace, and response times are faster than ever. However, it's important to use technology wisely to enhance the customer experience, not hinder it. Chatbots are an example of technology used to lower response times and help customers navigate your website more efficiently. However, as much as chatbots are an excellent tool, human interaction cannot be entirely replaced.

Measuring and Improving Customer Satisfaction

Measuring customer satisfaction helps businesses understand their customers' needs and pain points, leading to better customer service experiences. Customers who aren't heard become a significant problem. Creating methods to gather feedback from customers is vital to ensure that customer sentiment is collected and used to improve the quality of customer service. Utilizing surveys and NPS scores is a great way to gauge customer satisfaction levels.

Staying up-to-date with Changes in Customer Service Trends

The customer service landscape is always changing, and it's essential to stay current with new trends, tools, and technology to use customer service efficiently. With more and more communication channels available to customers, businesses need to stay agile and adapt to the new communication channels. Omni-channel support, two-way texting, and social listening are significant trends that businesses should be aware of.

Avoiding Common Customer Service Mistakes

Businesses make customer service mistakes more often than they should. One mistake is assuming customers are satisfied because they haven't complained. Another error is putting too much emphasis on policies and procedures and forgetting how these policies impact customers and their experience with the company. It's essential to avoid common mistakes and instead focus on achieving a positive customer experience consistently.

Conclusion

Ultimately, in business, the customer is the king. The best way to keep customers is to provide excellent customer service. Even when things go wrong, exemplary customer service can often be

MARKETING SUCCESS SECRETS

the turning point from customers being unhappy and becoming lifelong customers and advocates of your business. A well-crafted customer service strategy should be flexible enough to adapt to emerging technologies and changing trends in the market while remaining committed to putting customers first.

CHAPTER 19:
ANALYTICS AND
MEASUREMENT FOR
MAXIMUM IMPACT

Marketing is more than just creating compelling campaigns and content. It's also about understanding how those efforts impact your business. This is where analytics and measurement come in. Proper analytics can help you determine the success of your marketing campaigns, areas where you need to improve, and where your budget dollars are well spent.

Understanding the Importance of Analytics and Measurement

Analytics and measurement are an essential part of any marketing strategy. They allow you to measure the success of your efforts, understand your audience, and make data-driven decisions. Without a proper framework for analytics, it's difficult to know which of your marketing campaigns are effective and which ones need improvement.

Choosing the Right Analytics Tools for Your Business

When it comes to analytics tools, there's no shortage of options. From Google Analytics to HubSpot and other proprietary analytics tools, the key is to choose a tool that is easy to use, provides the data you need, and integrates well with your other marketing tools.

Before choosing a tool, consider the specific metrics that matter most to your business. Whether it's click-through rates, conversion rates, or social media engagement, ensure that your chosen tool provides that data.

Setting and Tracking Marketing KPIs

Before launching any marketing campaign, it's essential to establish Key Performance Indicators (KPIs). KPIs are metrics that help you measure success, and they should be tied to business goals.

When setting KPIs, ensure they are specific, measurable, attainable, relevant, and time-bound (SMART). This enables you to monitor your progress and make changes in real-time.

Analyzing Marketing Performance Across All Channels

With powerful analytics tools, you can track marketing performance across all channels, from social media to email marketing and beyond. This allows you to understand where your leads and conversions are coming from, the ROI on each channel, and areas where you need to focus your efforts.

Utilizing A/B Testing and Experimentation

A/B testing is a powerful technique that allows you to test different versions of your marketing campaigns to see which performs better. By testing two versions of the same campaign, you're able to determine which version delivers better results.

To get the most out of A/B testing, ensure that you have a large enough sample size and that you're only testing one variable at a time. This allows you to isolate the variable that's causing the performance difference.

Making Data-Driven Marketing Decisions

Data is critical when it comes to making marketing decisions. Analyzing data from your campaigns enables you to make informed decisions that are based on data rather than assumptions or gut feelings.

When making decisions, use data to understand what's working and what isn't. Use insights from analytics and measurement to optimize your campaigns, tweak your messaging, and adjust your budget as needed.

Staying Up-To-Date with Changes in Analytics and Measurement Trends

The field of analytics and measurement is always evolving, so it's essential to stay up-to-date with the latest trends and technologies. By doing so, you can ensure that you're taking advantage of the newest advancements and techniques to optimize your marketing campaigns.

Stay informed through industry publications, attending webinars, and conferences. As you adopt new tools and tactics, ensure that they integrate seamlessly with your current marketing stack.

Avoiding Common Analytics and Measurement Mistakes

While analytics and measurement can provide valuable insights, it's essential to steer clear of common mistakes. One mistake is failing to establish KPIs, which can make it difficult to measure success. Another is failing to test campaigns, which can result in missed opportunities.

Ensure that you collect quality data, prioritize metrics that matter to your business, and interpret your data properly. Avoid over-analyzing data to the point that it freezes the decision-making process.

Conclusion

Analytics and measurement are critical to the success of your marketing campaigns. With proper analytics, you're able to monitor performance, track KPIs, and make data-driven decisions that drive business growth. By understanding the importance of analytics and measurement, adopting the right tools, and avoiding common mistakes, you can optimize your marketing campaigns and achieve long-term success.

CHAPTER 20:
CONTINUOUSLY
INNOVATING
FOR LONG-TERM
MARKETING SUCCESS

Innovation is the key to long-term marketing success. As the business environment changes rapidly, marketers must adapt and innovate to stay ahead of the competition. Continuously innovating is not just about coming up with new and creative marketing ideas - it is about creating a culture of innovation, encouraging experimentation, and staying up-to-date with changes in marketing trends and technologies.

Embrace a Culture of Innovation

Innovation begins with company culture. To encourage innovation, businesses must create an environment that allows employees to be creative, take risks, and experiment with new ideas. One way to create a culture of innovation is by encouraging cross-functional collaboration. When employees from different departments come together to solve problems, they bring unique perspectives and approaches that can lead to innovative solutions.

Another way to foster a culture of innovation is by recognizing and rewarding innovative behaviors. This could mean setting up an innovation award program or integrating innovation into performance evaluations. Employees who are recognized and rewarded for their innovative ideas are more likely to continue to think outside the box and bring fresh ideas to the table.

Encourage New Ideas and Experimentation

To stay ahead of the competition, businesses must be willing to experiment with new ideas and marketing strategies. This means testing new channels, trying new tactics, and analyzing the results to determine what works and what doesn't. One way to experiment with new ideas is by conducting A/B testing. By testing two different versions of a marketing campaign, businesses can determine which version performs better and make data-driven decisions for future campaigns.

Another way to encourage experimentation is by utilizing agile marketing. Agile marketing is a flexible and iterative approach that allows businesses to quickly test and adjust their marketing strategies based on real-time data. Agile marketing involves breaking down tasks into small, manageable chunks, prioritizing tasks based on their impact, and collaborating in cross-functional teams.

Keep Up-to-Date with Changes in Marketing Trends and Technologies

Marketing trends and technologies are constantly evolving, and businesses must stay up-to-date to remain competitive. This means investing in education and professional development opportunities for marketing teams, attending industry conferences and events, and keeping a close eye on emerging marketing trends and technologies.

One emerging trend in marketing is machine learning and artificial intelligence. Machine learning algorithms can help businesses analyze vast amounts of data and make precise predictions about consumer behavior. Another emerging trend is augmented reality, which enables businesses to create immersive brand experiences and interactive marketing campaigns. By keeping up-to-date with changes in marketing trends and technologies, businesses can stay ahead of the curve and gain a competitive edge.

Constantly Analyze and Improve Marketing Efforts

Continuous improvement is a critical element of long-term marketing success. Businesses must constantly analyze their marketing efforts, identify areas for improvement, and make data-driven decisions to optimize their strategies. This means analyzing data from various sources, such as social media analytics, web analytics, and customer feedback, to gain a holistic view of marketing performance.

Businesses can use a variety of tools to analyze marketing performance, such as key performance indicators (KPIs), dashboards, and data visualization tools. By monitoring KPIs, businesses can determine whether their marketing efforts are aligned with their goals and make adjustments as needed. Dashboards and data visualization tools can help teams make sense of complex data sets and identify patterns and trends over time.

Embrace Failure as a Learning Opportunity

Innovation requires risk-taking, and risk-taking means that failure is a possibility. However, failure is not necessarily a bad thing - it can be a learning opportunity that leads to future success. Businesses must create a culture that embraces failure as a learning opportunity, rather than a source of shame or blame.

One way to embrace failure is by conducting retrospective meetings. After a marketing campaign or project ends, teams should come together to analyze what went well, what didn't go so well, and what can be improved next time. By openly discussing failures and identifying areas for improvement, teams can learn from their mistakes and apply those learnings to future marketing efforts.

Build a Long-Term Marketing Strategy for Sustained Success

Long-term marketing success requires a strategic approach that aligns with the wider business goals. Businesses must develop a marketing plan that outlines a clear vision for their brand, defines their target audience, and outlines the tactics and channels needed to achieve their goals. The marketing plan should be flexible enough to adapt to changing market conditions, but it should also provide a roadmap for sustained success.

Staying Ahead of the Competition through Innovation

Innovation is the key to staying ahead of the competition in today's fast-paced business environment. By creating a culture of innovation, encouraging experimentation, staying up-to-date with changes in marketing trends and technologies, constantly analyzing and improving marketing efforts, embracing failure as a learning opportunity, and building a long-term marketing strategy.

Final Thoughts

In conclusion, building a successful marketing strategy is an ever-evolving process that requires creativity, hard work and flexibility. As we have seen throughout this book, there are many different tools and tactics you can use to promote your brand and reach your target audience. However, the most important factor in achieving marketing success is having a deep understanding of your customers' needs and preferences.

Remember to always test and measure the effectiveness of your marketing campaigns, so you can learn from both successes and failures. Don't be afraid to try new things and take risks, but also be prepared to adjust your approach based on feedback from your audience.

Finally, don't forget the importance of building strong relationships with your customers. This means providing them with value beyond just your products or services. Engage with them through social media channels, respond to their feedback and questions promptly, and reward their loyalty with special offers or exclusive content.

By following these key principles and implementing the actionable strategies outlined in this book, you will be well on your way to achieving marketing success for your business.

Good luck!

ABOUT THE AUTHOR

Ray Goodwin

Ray Goodwin, is the author behind this series of captivating books on Business Development and self improvement, and has left an indelible mark on the field. He was born and raised in the bustling city of London, where he developed a strong work ethic and an insatiable curiosity about the inner workings of successful businesses. Throughout his illustrious career, Ray leveraged his extensive knowledge and experience to help numerous companies flourish and prosper.

His keen insights and innovative strategies has earned him recognition, driving him to share his expertise with others. Ray believes in the power of sharing knowledge to elevate businesses and empower aspiring entrepreneurs.

Ray's dedication to his craft is evident in the numerous books he has authored on business development and self improvement. His writing style seamlessly blends practical advice, thought-provoking concepts, and real-life case studies, making his books invaluable resources for business professionals and novices alike. His ability to distill complex concepts into accessible language has greatly impacted the lives and careers of countless individuals.

Now retired from the corporate world, Ray and his beloved wife have settled in the idyllic English countryside. Surrounded by the beauty of nature, Ray finds inspiration for his writing and indulges in his hobbies.

Ray Goodwin's books continue to serve as enduring guides for those seeking success in the business world. With a wealth of experience and a deep understanding of the inner workings of businesses, Ray's work remains a testament to his passion for sharing knowledge and helping others flourish.